T·H·E
HUMMINGBIRDS' GIFT

STEFAN CZERNECKI AND TIMOTHY RHODES
Illustrated by Stefan Czernecki

Straw Weavings by Juliana Reyes de Silva and Juan Hilario Silva

HAMPTON-BROWN BOOKS
MANY CULTURES, MANY LANGUAGES…MANY POSSIBILITIES!™

More hummingbirds than one could ever count come to drink nectar from the beautiful flowers that flourish around the village of Tzintzuntzan. In fact, that's how this Mexican village got its name; Tzintzuntzan (pronounced *TSEENT soont SAHN*) is the Tarascan Indian name that means "the place of the hummingbirds." The birds are legendary there, for they once performed a great service.

3

Many years ago, a farmer named Isidro lived on the outskirts of Tzintzuntzan with his wife, Consuelo, and their three small children.

Every morning the family would rise at the rooster's first call and go to work side by side in their wheat fields. They cared for their crop until it was ripe and ready to be harvested. When all of the wheat was cut, they sold it to the nearby mill.

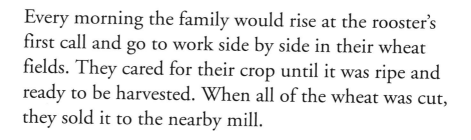

One year Isidro and Consuelo planted the seeds as usual for a new crop of wheat. Day after day they searched the sky for rain clouds, but none could be seen. From dawn until dusk the sun shone bright and hot in the sky.

Isidro watched the spindly stalks of wheat in the parched earth slowly wither and turn into yellow straw.

Even the hardy cacti growing around the farm turned brown and brittle. The river dried up.

All the flowers withered as well, and the hummingbirds could not find nectar to drink. Many died. "Poor little birds," Consuelo said to Isidro. "We must find a way to help them."

13

Together they devised a plan. Isidro took the burro and two large clay jars and followed the dry river bed to the lake, which still held a small amount of water. There he filled the jars.

When Isidro returned home, Consuelo carefully mixed the water with clay to mold tiny pots in the shape of flowers. She baked the pots in the sun, and then she and the children painted them with all the bright colors that were once in the garden.

Next Consuelo mixed sugar with the remainder of the water and poured the sweet nectar into the clay containers.

The children placed the painted containers in the branches of the bushes around the garden. Soon a blur of wings surrounded the pots, and the hummingbirds drank their fill.

Isidro struggled to bring fresh water from the lake every day. Consuelo mixed the sweet nectar, and the children made sure the pots were always filled. The hummingbirds were saved!

But as Consuelo watched her children with the little birds, she began to worry. The hummingbirds now had something to eat, but how would she feed her children? There was no wheat to sell and hardly any food in the cupboard.

The hummingbirds, sensing her anxiety, flew out of
the bushes and spread over the dusty field like an
iridescent blanket. Each bird was a whirl of activity
as it gathered a few small bits of straw in its beak and
flew back toward Consuelo. When a small pile
had formed, the birds settled at her feet and began
to work.

As Consuelo looked on, the little birds darted about,
weaving the bits of straw into beautiful tiny figures.

Consuelo called to Isidro and the children. "What a blessing this is," she said excitedly. "See how the hummingbirds have shown us what to do!"

She asked Isidro and the children to gather all the straw from the fields and to pile it in the shade by the front porch. Then Consuelo showed them how to weave the figures.

Day and night they wove. Soon the pile of straw was transformed into tiny dancers, musicians, skeletons, and many other shapes.

"We will sell the figures at the Day of the Dead festival!" Isidro proclaimed. "All the villagers will gather in the town square to eat, talk, and explore the marketplace. They will be buying gifts to give to their children and to honor the dead."

On the morning before the festival, the family took their straw figures to the village to sell.

The square was soon crowded with people, and everyone stopped to admire the woven figures. Isidro and Consuelo sold all of them quickly and earned enough money to last all year!

They bought sweets for the children and food, flowers, and candles for the festival.

At midnight, the family joined the rest of the villagers in the procession to the cemetery. There they cleaned their ancestors' graves and placed flowers on the headstones. Then they told the children stories about their grandparents and great-grandparents.

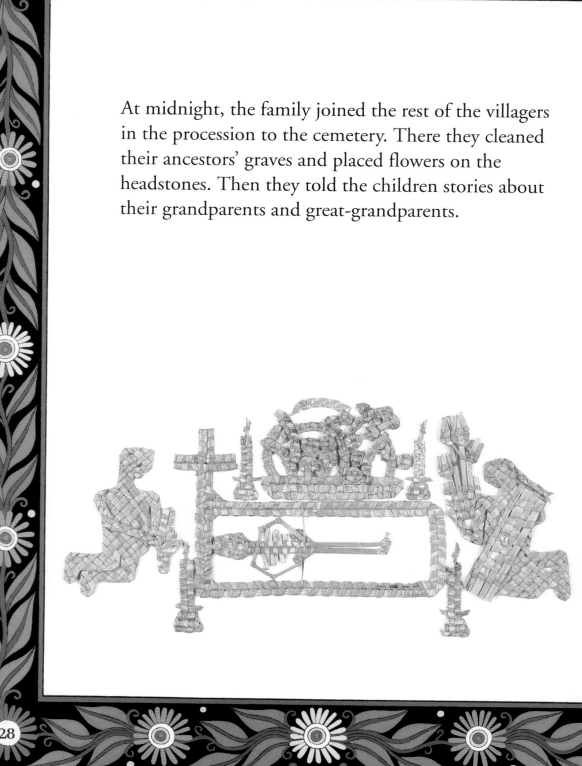

Several weeks later it began to rain. The family laughed and sang because they knew the river would be full again. The wheat would grow and the flowers would blossom for the hummingbirds.

Every year after that, Isidro, Consuelo, and their children wove the straw and displayed the tiny figures. And to this day their children's children and *their* children remember the hummingbirds' gift.

Authors' note: Tzintzuntzan, Mexico—once the capital of the powerful Tarascan empire—is today a small village near the ruins of the *yácatas,* the pre-Columbian pyramids destroyed by the Spanish conquistadores when they conquered this area of Mexico in the 1520s. The Spanish introduced wheat, and the Tarascan Indians, already acquainted with weaving, used the straw to weave figures called *panicuas* that could be used for various holidays.

One of these holidays is the Day of the Dead, celebrated on November 2 throughout Mexico. It is a day of special significance in the folklore of the country. The symbol of the holiday is Death, portrayed as a skeleton or skull. It is not a tribute to the macabre but rather an exultation of life. The symbol is seen everywhere: on costumes in the marketplace and on specially made candies, called sugar skulls, usually bearing the name of the departed. Families clean and decorate the burial places of their relatives, arranging food and flowers on the graves. A processional to the cemetery begins at midnight on November 1, the eve of the Day of the Dead. Families gather around the graves, playing host to the dead, who are said to return for one night. Children listen to stories about their ancestors, and the oral history of the people is passed along to the next generation.

For Joyce and Brian Renton

Text copyright © 1994 by Stefan Czernecki and Timothy Rhodes.
Illustrations copyright © 1994 by Stefan Czernecki.
By arrangement with Hyperion Books for Children.

Hampton-Brown Books
P.O. Box 223220
Carmel, California 93922
(800) 333-3510

Printed in the United States of America.

ISBN 1-56334-720-2

96 97 98 99 00 01 02 03 04 10 9 8 7 6 5 4 3 2

The artwork for each picture is prepared using gouache.
This book is set in 16-point Garamond.